Hieroglyphics

by Grace Hansen

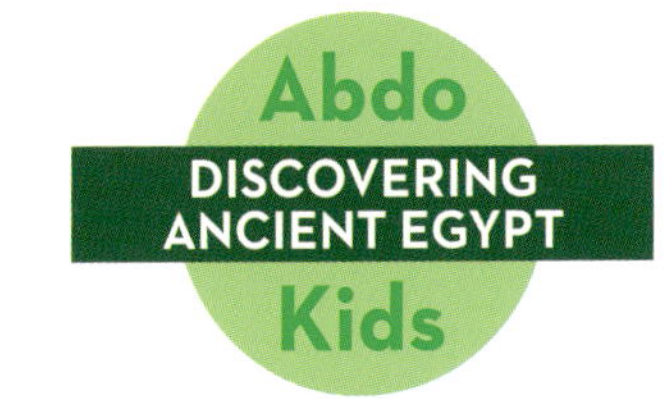

Abdo Kids Jumbo is an Imprint of Abdo Kids
abdobooks.com

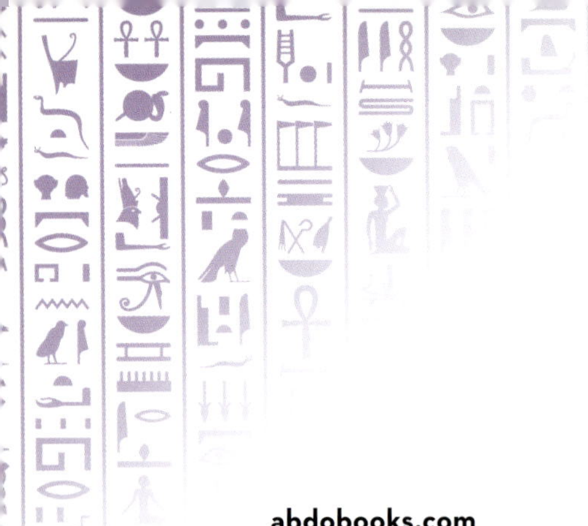

abdobooks.com

Published by Abdo Kids, a division of ABDO, P.O. Box 398166, Minneapolis, Minnesota 55439.

Printed in the United States of America, North Mankato, Minnesota.

102023

012024

Photo Credits: Alamy, Getty Images, Shutterstock, ©British Museum p1/CC BY-NC-SA 4.0, ©Peter Roan p13/CC BY-NC 2.0, ©Jeff Dahl p19/CC BY-SA 4.0

Production Contributors: Teddy Borth, Jennie Forsberg, Grace Hansen
Design Contributors: Victoria Bates, Candice Keimig

Library of Congress Control Number: 2023937678

Publisher's Cataloging-in-Publication Data

Names: Hansen, Grace, author.

Title: Hieroglyphics / by Grace Hansen

Description: Minneapolis, Minnesota : Abdo Kids, 2024 | Series: Discovering ancient Egypt | Includes online resources and index.

Identifiers: ISBN 9781098268459 (lib. bdg.) | ISBN 9781098269159 (ebook) | ISBN 9781098269500 (Read-to-Me ebook)

Subjects: LCSH: Hieroglyphics--Juvenile literature. | Inscriptions, Egyptian--Juvenile literature. | Ideography--Juvenile literature.

Classification: DDC 932--dc23

Table of Contents

Record Keepers

Writing was very important to the ancient Egyptians. It was even considered **sacred**.

5

Egyptian **scribes** had plenty to write about. They wrote medical and religious texts. They wrote lists, recipes, and stories.

Surfaces & Tools

Scribes wrote on almost any surface. **Papyrus** rolls, coffins, statues, temples, and walls were all available.

The ancient Egyptians wrote by pressing a tool into a clay tablet. They formed pictures called hieroglyphs. This style of writing began in around 3500 BCE.

Clay was free to use. **Scribes** could reuse tablets that had not been baked. They did this by wetting the clay and rubbing out the letters.

13

Symbols

Early hieroglyphic script used symbols to represent words and word sounds. However, the Egyptians never created an alphabet.

Scribes used 600 to 700 hieroglyphs regularly. They used this type of writing mainly for religious texts. Some of the symbols were especially important.

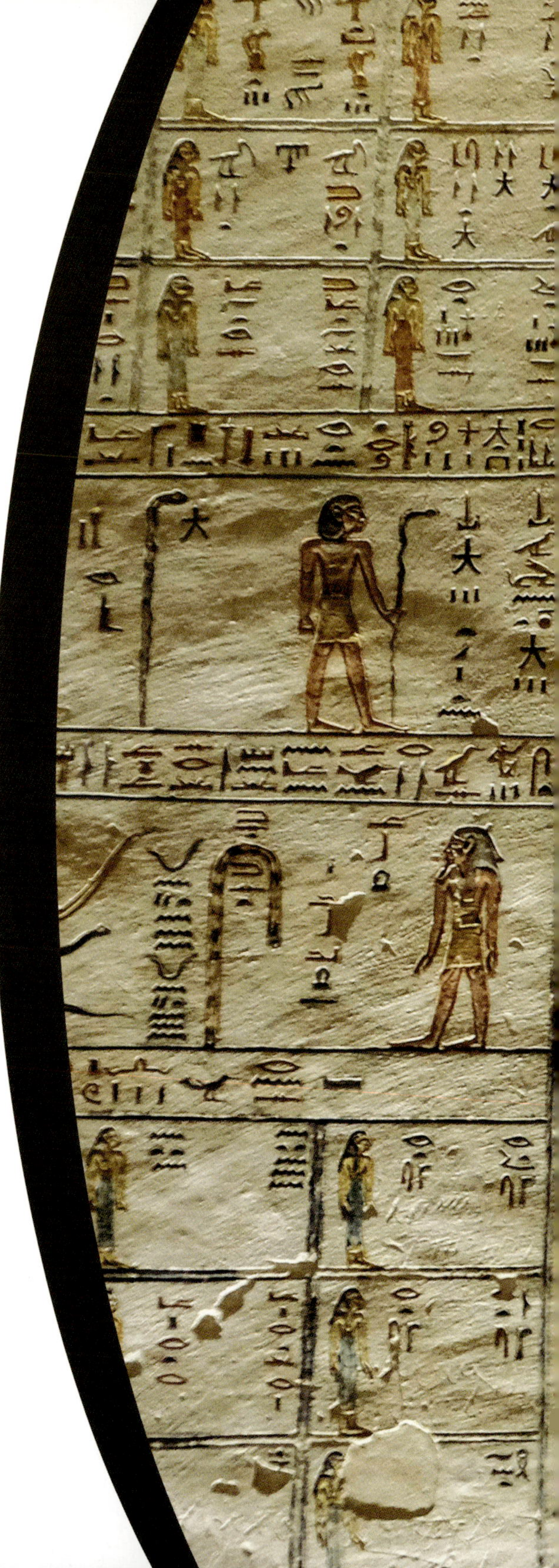

The Eye of Horus was said to protect people. Egyptians used it protect against **envy**, disease, and evil.

The scarab beetle was a symbol of death, rebirth, and power. It was said to guide and protect people in the afterlife. Both living and dead Egyptians often wore the scarab beetle.

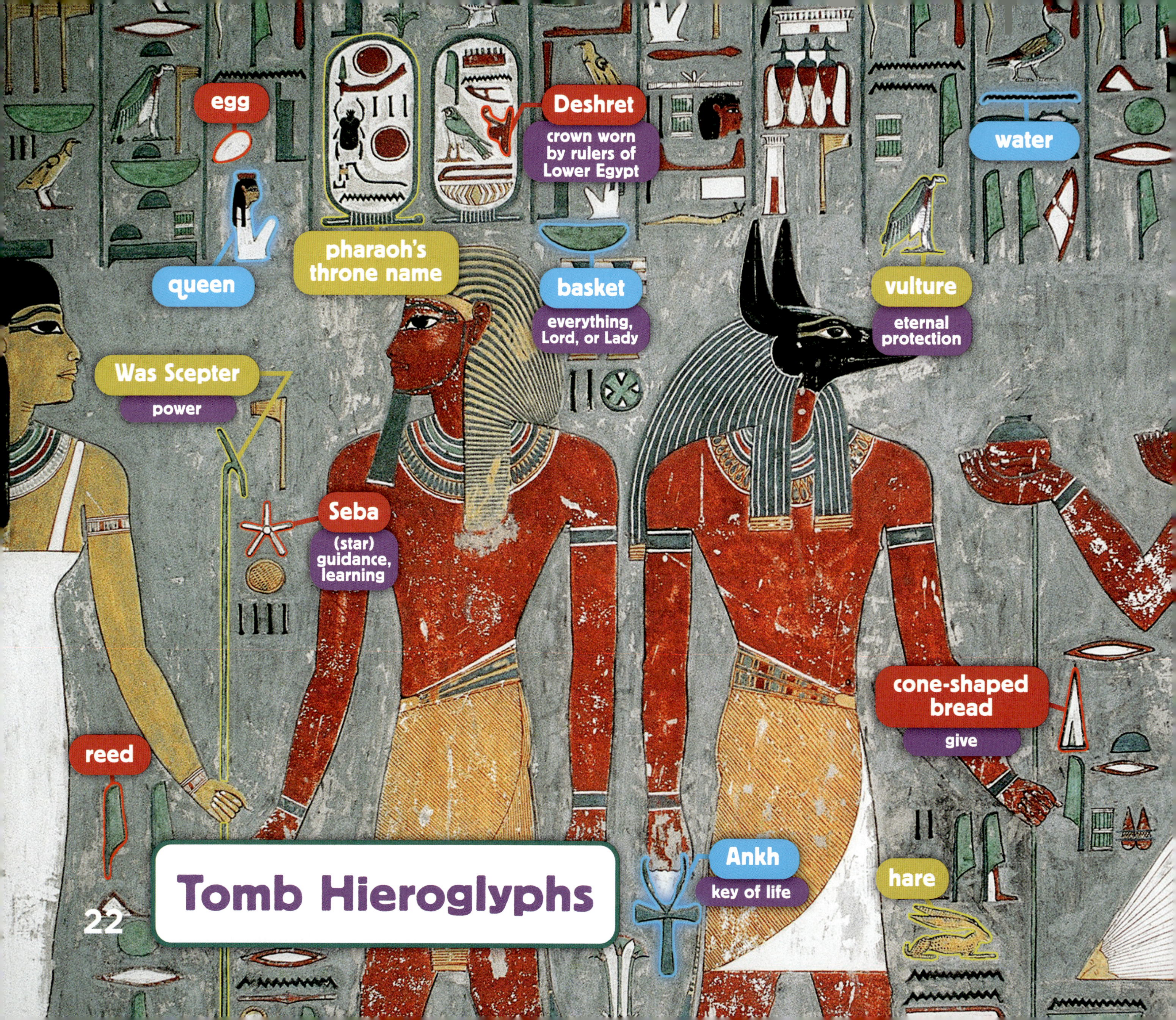

Tomb Hieroglyphs

Glossary

envy – a feeling of wanting what someone else has.

papyrus – a tall water plant of the Nile valley in Egypt.

sacred – holy and connected with the gods.

scribe – in ancient Egypt, a person whose job was to write about everyday life and extraordinary happenings. Scribes were highly educated writers and record keepers.

Index